CHOOSING
SIDES

by Philip Hewes
illustrated by Shirley Beckes

Harcourt
SCHOOL PUBLISHERS

Printed in China

ISBN 10: 0-15-351449-3
ISBN 13: 978-0-15-351449-4

Ordering Options
ISBN 10: 0-15-351213-X (Grade 3 Advanced Collection)
ISBN 13: 978-0-15-351213-1 (Grade 3 Advanced Collection)
ISBN 10: 0-15-358085-2 (package of 5)
ISBN 13: 978-0-15-358085-7 (package of 5)

2 3 4 5 6 7 8 9 10 985 12 11 10 09 08 07

"We are the champions!" Alison sang loudly.

"You played well today, and I'm extremely proud of you," said Mom.

"Thanks, and just wait until I tell Sarah. She'll be so jealous," replied Alison.

Mom sighed, "I'm certain Sarah also had a very good game."

They pulled into the parking lot next to the field where Sarah was laughing with other members of her team. She waved good-bye and climbed into the back seat next to Alison, tossing her bag of soccer equipment onto the floor between them.

"We are the champions!" Alison sang happily at Sarah.

"You can't be because the championship hasn't even been played yet," replied Sarah.

"Well, we're in the semifinals," announced Alison.

"How was your game, Sarah?" asked Mom.

"We won," shrugged Sarah, "as expected."

Alison sat silently for a moment, thinking about Sarah's team.

"When do you play next, Sarah?" asked Mom.

"We play on Saturday at one," said Sarah.

"So do we," replied Alison.

There was a brief pause as they realized that they were playing against each other! Then they began to argue about who was going to win the game.

Mom said in a soothing voice, "I'm glad that you both played well and that both of your teams won. It would be nice, though, if you two could congratulate each other and wish each other luck."

Without looking at each other, Alison and Sarah both murmured, "Congratulations and good luck."

"I'm certainly glad that for once Dad and I are going to be able to watch both of you play," said Mom.

The girls often had games at the same time, so Mom and Dad usually took turns going to one or the other's games.

"Who do you want to win?" asked Alison.

"Yes, who are you going to root for?" asked Sarah.

There was a tiny moment of silence from the front seat. Then Mom said calmly, "I hope you both play well, and I'll root for both of you."

"Which side are you going to sit on?" asked Sarah.

"You should sit on my side because we've never gotten this far in the tournament, and Sarah's team won championships last year and the year before," announced Alison.

"That's not fair because next year I have to move to a different age group, and my team is breaking up. I may never win again," replied Sarah.

"I just hope that you both play well, and let's not worry about it anymore," replied Mom wearily.

The car stopped in their driveway, and both girls went straight into the house without saying a word to each other.

Later, Alison was doing her homework when she heard a strange bouncing sound. Alison narrowed her eyes because she knew that sound—Sarah was practicing with a soccer ball in her room. Alison tried to concentrate on her math for a moment but then gave up.

"Someone must need an awful lot of practice," Alison announced very loudly.

The bouncing stopped, and Alison smiled and went back to work.

During the next few days, Alison and Sarah didn't play together like they usually did. Each of them spoke to their parents in private, trying to find out which team they wanted to win the game. Neither Mom nor Dad would give a straight answer. They only praised each girl's skills and said encouraging words about playing well in Saturday's game.

On Friday, Mom discovered Alison in the laundry room, digging through a pile of clean clothes.

"What are you looking for in here, Alison?" Mom asked.

"I can't find my lucky soccer socks, and I desperately need them for the game tomorrow," wailed Alison.

Mom chuckled, "Oh, Alison, lucky socks don't matter."

"You're just saying that because you don't want me to win!" Alison cried.

"Honey, I just meant that you play well enough that you don't need lucky socks, and of course I want you to win. How can I make you understand that?" said Mom.

"Promise you'll cheer for me, not Sarah," sobbed Alison.

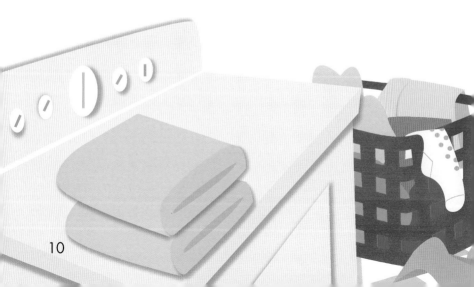

"I can't promise you that, but I told you already, I just want you both to play well and have fun," said Mom.

"Sarah's team always wins," Alison replied.

"Sarah's team has more experience, but you and your team are doing very well, and everyone realizes that," replied Mom.

"I just want to be the one who wins for once," Alison whispered.

"You will, if not tomorrow, then someday," said Mom.

Alison hugged Mom and slowly walked to her room. "I hope tomorrow is someday," Alison thought.

On Saturday, the whole family went to the game.

"Where should we look for you?" asked Alison.

"Don't worry, they'll be sitting on your side because everybody wants you to win because they feel sorry for you," Sarah said dramatically.

"Sarah!" said Mom. "You know that we—"

"—want you both to play well," Alison and Sarah said together.

They looked at each other and, for the first time in days, were actually chuckling together.

"Good luck," Sarah said.

"Good luck to you," replied Alison.

During warm up, Alison glanced into the crowd on her side, and there was Mom! Then Alison looked at the other side where Dad was in the crowd for Sarah's team. At halftime, they switched places.

It was a very close game. Alison's team was down 2-1 with three minutes to play when Alison scored to tie the game!

Then, as time ran out, Sarah dribbled the ball towards the goal, passed the ball, and her teammate kicked the ball into the goal. The game was over, and Sarah's team had won.

13

Alison and Sarah each made plans to meet their friends for parties later and then found their parents.

Mom hugged Sarah, then Alison. "You were both fantastic!"

"You know, you're actually better than I was at your age," Sarah said to Alison.

Alison brightened. "Really?"

Sarah nodded and said seriously, "I was impressed, and I bet you'll win next year."

"I hope so," said Alison. "Now let's go because I want to get to the party!"

"Me, too!" replied Sarah.

Think Critically

1. What is the problem in the story?

2. Which team wins the game?

3. How would you describe Alison?

4. Do you think Alison and Sarah usually get along? Why or why not?

5. Since her team had never won, do you think that Alison's parents should have rooted for her to win? Why or why not?

 **Social Studies**

Sports Around the World Alison and Sarah play soccer. Find out about soccer and other sports that are played around the world, and make a chart showing where different sports are played.

School-Home Connection Find a family member or friend who grew up with a brother or sister. Ask whether there were times when they competed for the same thing and how they handled it.

Word Count: 1,016